STACY AVALOS

LEARNING TO FIND PEACE AFTER LOSS BOOK

Finding Peace, Happiness & Purpose While Surviving Grief

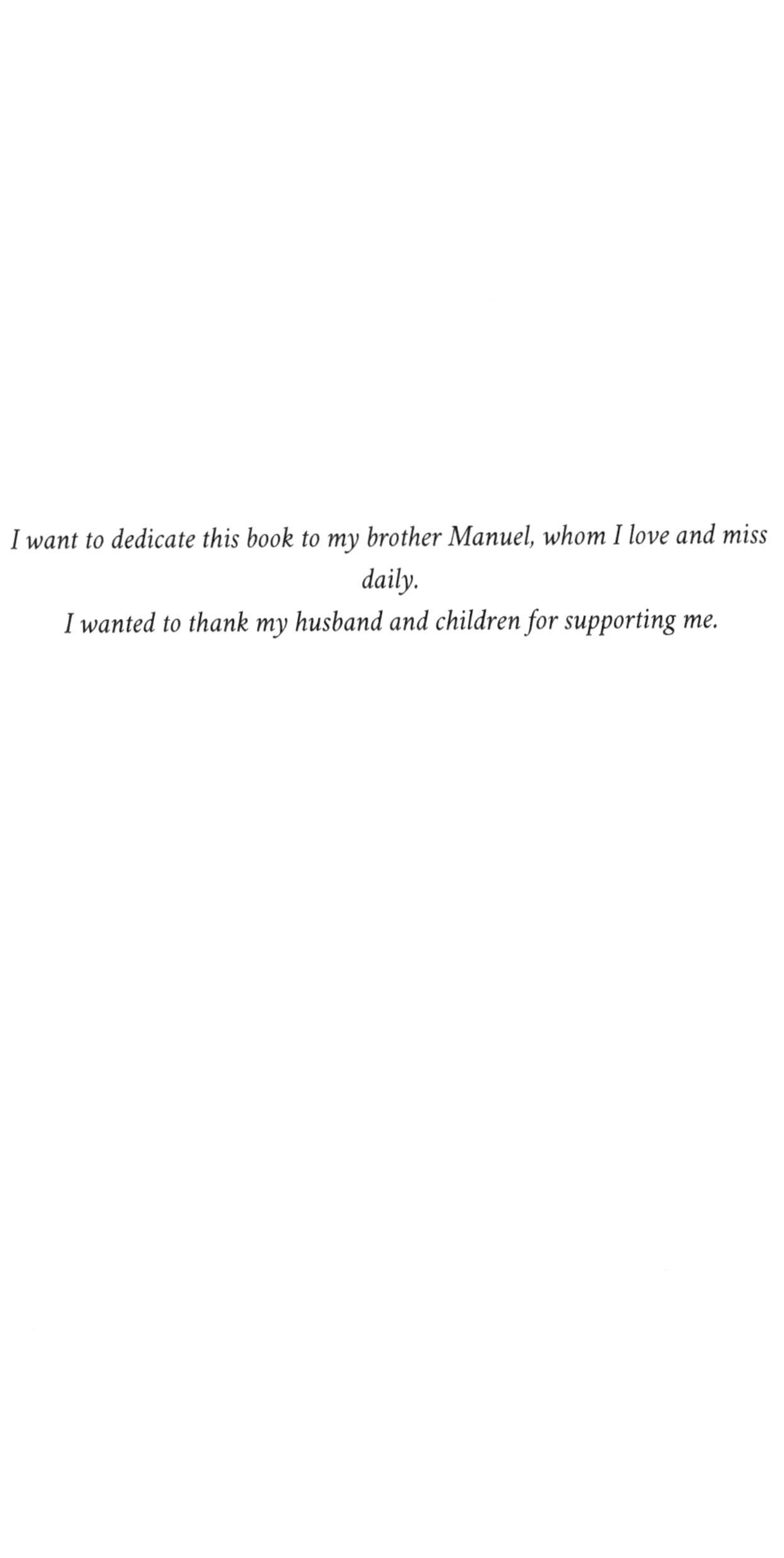

I want to dedicate this book to my brother Manuel, whom I love and miss daily.
I wanted to thank my husband and children for supporting me.

Contents

I

Part One

"There is a sacredness in tears. They are not the mark of weakness, but of power. They speak more eloquently than ten thousand tongues. They are the messengers of overwhelming grief, of deep contrition, and of unspeakable love."
- Washington Irving as posted on MyGriefAssist.com

1

Introduction

Welcome to Learning to Find Peace After Loss. If you are here, then most likely, like myself, you have experienced the loss of a loved one. We will be walking through different stages of grief, how to recognize where you may be, and ways to help you find peace and happiness again. You will also see there are many, many, many different types of grief, and everyone deals with it in their own way. You can be grieving the loss of a spouse, parent, sibling, or child. Many don't realize there are other types of grief out there. There is grief in divorce, letting go of someone close to you, losing a pet, or even having a child leave home. You will come across people telling you how to grieve or that you shouldn't be grieving any longer. Your feelings are valid; they are your own, and having someone tell you any different will not change how you think.

All I am here to do is share my experiences, my relationship with loss, and all the crazy feelings that came with my journey. To say that I have gotten over my grief would be a lie. There will always be triggers & events that will bring those emotions flooding back, but I have come out the other side of the deep depression, the feelings of being forsaken, and

I have found a sense of inner peace. I have SURVIVED!!! Just writing this has brought on the tears, but it is not tears that are coming from fear or sadness anymore. With that said, I kiss my two fingers, raise them to the sky, and say, "PEACE BROTHER, YOU ARE LOVED AND MISSED." Sometimes life gets crazy and hectic, and you don't realize that the feelings are just on the surface. I needed that cry and am not ashamed to say that anymore.

With all of that said, let's leap into our journey together. Yes, you heard me. TOGETHER. I need to write this just as much as I think others going through loss may need to listen to it.

2

What Is Grief & Why Do I Feel Like This

What in the heck is grief??? I mean what it is and why we go through it. I had many days asking myself, why do I feel like this? I knew this day was coming; my brother had been sick for a long time. I tried to distance myself from him for a bit, hoping the pain would not come when he passed. I was wrong, really wrong. That distance, even for not long, caused me more remorse than I could ever imagine.

GRIEF is pain, sorrow, anger, just this tremendous emotional loss of someone you loved. It leaves you raw and your heart forever changed. It is a pain unlike anything I have ever felt in my life. There were days I thought I would never want to leave my bed. Days that I cried so much that I lost my voice. I wandered through my life those first few months like I was the one that was gone like I was a ghost in my own life. Going through life like this is crazy because I have children, but you cannot control grief no matter how much you try. You need to take that ride and know you will be okay once you get to the other side. I am not saying that you will one day wake up and forget your loved one or how much they meant to you. No, not at all. I am just saying time and going through the process of grief, the days will get easier, your heart and mind will heal, and you will be so much stronger than you ever imagined you could be. I think of my big brother every single day. Some days are easier than others.

No one can bypass the grieving process. Take it one day at a time, and little by little, you will begin to mend, but only when you let yourself grieve. Grief is not only a mental or emotional process; it also affects your physical health. There were days I didn't want to eat, sleep, let alone brush my hair or shower. My body just ached everywhere. Maybe that sounds extreme, but it is true. Then there were days my heart was hurting so bad all I wanted to do was sleep cause there, in my dreams, my brother was alive and healthy. But it wasn't real, and waking up to feel that loss again was excruciating. I am happy to say I no longer have that overwhelming feeling of despair. I am in a place of peace and happiness that took time. I had to realize I was still grieving for many months after and that I needed to work on finding peace. I know my brother would not have wanted me to suffer or for him to be the cause of my sadness and pain.

You may have heard this many times, but I will repeat it. The grieving process is different for everyone. Everyone's experiences are different. We are not all the same; there is no such thing as being normal, so why try to force your grief into this tidy little box and hide it away when you think you have met some deadline for your suffering? Some people may grieve over weeks and months, while others can take years to repent. Let your heart guide you. You will start having days when you feel like I can do this. I can make it through this day without crying. I can get out of bed and get dressed. These little steps eventually help lead you to the other side of grief. Once you get there, you will learn to let in the peace and allow yourself to feel happiness again. So feel it, let it all in so you can learn to let go.

3

The Denial Is Real, My Friends

There is something that happens to your mental state when you are grieving. Until you have experienced loss, you think about how people could be in denial that someone has passed away. I mean, logic tells you that if you were like myself and saw your loved one up close when they passed, they are gone. You have the doctors who told you, and you have other loved ones experiencing loss along with you. It seems that all of that logic is out the window.

Here is where my experience led me. When my aunt told me my brother had passed, I rushed to the hospital. I remember my husband driving me there, but I don't really remember the drive or even getting out of the car, walking through the hospital parking lot, and taking the elevator to his floor. I remember running into his room and seeing my aunt holding onto my mother, trying to console her while crying and dealing with her pain. I threw my arms around my brother in that hospital bed, holding onto him, and prayed that this couldn't happen. If I hold onto him and do not let go, it won't be real, and I won't have to let him go. I don't remember how long I held onto him, but I remember not wanting to let go. I remember the doctor talking, but it was like all sound was blocked out. The rest of the day was a blur; even breaking the news to his children felt unreal. I woke up the following day thinking, okay, let me get up and get myself ready to see my brother in the hospital. I walked right into one of his children crying in the hallway. The pain came rushing back full force. I tried to push it all down and get through that day. Reliving this moment hurts, and the tears start flowing, but it will pass, and I am hoping my journey will help someone else going through this.

You go through this step of denial; well, maybe not everyone, but there is a lot that does. Like a ritual, my brother would call every Wednesday and Sunday to chat and catch up. Those days were hard as I would find me still waiting for his call. When my phone would ring, I would think I would hear his voice on the other end. Eventually, I tried just to shut down those feelings. Considering I have to be solid for my family and my brother's children, who are in total shock and immense pain. I kept thinking to myself, just let me get through the funeral planning and show a brave face to those around me. I would wake up forgetting that he had passed. He was my big brother and can't be gone because if he is gone, what is my purpose? I realized I am the oldest sibling now and thought, what does that even mean? Where is my place? Where do I fit in this life? I began to feel numb, pushing all the pressure and pain down daily. I was not allowing myself to go through the grieving process. I felt okay; you cried for a few weeks; get over yourself. You need to be solid for your family and push through. Be the example. Thinking back now, I was not a good example to anyone. Nor should I have tried to be. I should have let myself grieve. In turn, I showed everyone that expressing their grief was okay. Not bundle it up inside until one day it comes bursting out.

I went through a period of denial and numbness. I told myself if I pushed my brother's death deep down and made myself forget it, it didn't really happen. I woke up, brushed my hair, went to work, came home, took care of my kids, and went to bed. Repeat that over and over for months; that was my life. That doesn't sound wrong. I even turned my brother's prayer card over so I wouldn't see his face every day. I was walking through my life, but I was not living. Inside I knew all the hurt would resurface, but I always thought I would have time that it would be my choice when I would grieve, ha, like it was up to me. One day it all came bursting out while at work. I was listening to music while working. A song that my brother and I used to sing together growing up came on. "Steal My Sunshine," by Len. My brother used to call me his Sunshine. It brought me reeling back so fast that I did not see it coming.

I felt like I couldn't catch my breath. I had to tell my boss I needed to go home because it was about my brother. I am thankful I have a fantastic understanding boss. She let me take the rest of the day off. When I got to my vehicle, that was it. I completely lost it. I sat at work in the parking lot for over an hour, just crying, screaming, reliving the day I lost my brother over and over until I could finally catch my breath and head home. I hugged my kids. I finally broke down with my husband and let him know that I am grieving and I am not exactly sure how to make it stop or what to do. He let me know that he would be there for me. If I needed to be alone, let him know; if I needed more attention, let him know. I am telling you all this because you need to know that hiding from your grief and trying to run from it or push it down does not make it go away. The only way to get past the suffering is to deal with it, feel it and work through it. I tell you, denial and numbness were just the beginning for me. Next came anger, and with its exhaustion and brain fog.

4

How Can You Be Angry At Someone That's Gone?

Let me tell you, my friends; the anger came for me. I was getting over the denial and that feeling of emptiness. I feel like I woke up, and I was just pissed. I was so angry he made me feel this way. I was mad he left me. He was my big brother and was supposed to be there to look out for me. He broke his promise. He left me way too early. We used to talk about being old, being our weird selves. He made me feel like it was okay to be different, a bit odd, a nerd, or whatever. I felt like I could be myself and maybe even a bit crazy around him. He was the only one I could watch Star Wars with and nerd out. He was my friend and the one I went to with all my crap. I leaned on him, and he relied on me. He took that all away from me. He took away a part of my future. I was beyond mad. With madness comes some craziness, let me tell you. I turned that prayer card back over and yelled at him like he was still there. I told him he should be here with his kids. We should be watching our kids grow up together. I cursed at him; I looked to the sky and told him if he came back, I would kick his ass for what he was putting me through. I would raise my finger to the sky and flip him off more times than I remember.

With this anger for a while, I felt powerful, whereas I felt so weak before. There were days I felt ashamed of the rage. How could I feel angry at my brother for dying? I think it was because I felt abandoned. I was mad not just at him but at the unbearable pain it caused me. My life had changed, and I had no control over it. With this anger came extreme exhaustion and this brain fog I could not shake. I started mixing stuff up, and I began to stutter for a bit. (I don't think people noticed, but I did.) I would forget what I was talking about mid-sentence. I would just be sitting there staring into space, and for the life of me, I could not remember what I was thinking or doing. It was scary. At one point, I thought I might have had a stroke. Then the exhaustion set in, and I could barely peel myself out of bed.

I would get myself ready and head to work. I am sure my colleagues got tired of me saying how tired I was every day. (Best excuse, blame it on the kids. I am sure they also contributed to my exhaustion.) I would get home, take my shoes off, say hello to my children and fall asleep as soon as I hit the couch. I would only wake up to feed them, get them ready for bed, and then drag myself to bed to do it again the next day. On the weekends, I could sleep the whole day away. It wasn't until my husband told me that there had to be something wrong. You can't possibly be that tired. You slept for more than 10 hours. Then my son said it was like I was not even here. I am always sleeping. I knew I had to change, but first, I had to figure out what was happening.

I realized that I was holding on to all this anger, which was taking a toll. I was becoming burnt out. I didn't know what to do with that. I had to dig deeper. I had found I was not just mad at my brother but with myself. Let me explain. My brother had left me in charge when he went to the hospital. I still remember that last phone call. "Sissy," he said. "We need to talk; I am not doing good, and this time, there is a good chance I won't make it through surgery," I told him to stop talking like that. He would be fine. He then yelled, "I need you to listen to me! Really listen. I need you to watch over my babies. Make sure they are okay when I am gone. Make sure our little brother is okay, take care of dad, and don't let mom disappear. (another story some other time.) Tell Sissy Poo (our little sister) that I love her. Make sure you tell my sister I love her and I am sorry. (the middle sister) Make sure my kids know I love them and would be there if I could. He then got into the details. He told me he didn't want to be stuck on all these machines. He didn't want anyone to resuscitate him, he had been in too much pain for way too long, and although my brother didn't want to die, he knew it was coming. He told me he could not keep fighting. He couldn't handle the pain anymore. He asked not to be on life support and to ensure no one prolonged his suffering. He told me he was scared, really scared, and he cried. He felt like he had spent the past five years waiting for this day to come, and my brother felt like it was here and he wasn't ready for it. I tried to console him. The last thing he said to me was you will always be my Sunshine Sissy; I love you. That was the last time I would ever talk to my big brother.

The next day I got a call stating my brother's surgery was postponed, and it would not happen for at least another day. I thought maybe he had just decided not to do the surgery. I did not get a hold of him that day. His phone was off, and I found out later that he was meeting with church members and preparing himself. The day after was when I would get the call from the hospital. Doctors let me know my brother left me in charge of his health care decisions. The doctors advised that my brother was out of surgery but was not waking up. I panicked. Then I drove 3 hours to the hospital and was pulled over. (Not for speeding, calm down.) Finally, I made it there. We were there for days, with no progress. He got worse and worse. Then the day came when I had to make the decision. Taking my brother off of life support was the hardest decision of my life. People told me that you are killing him if you pull the plug. He can still come out of this. Miracles happen, but we will never know if you take him off life support. I knew what I was supposed to do and what my brother wanted. But I waited; I waited 14 days before making that decision. The doctors came to us and told us the next steps. We can only keep him on a ventilator for 14 days, and then we will have to put a trach in him. He has already had one infection, and he is susceptible to more infections with a trach. His major organs were shutting down, and all I was doing was prolonging the inevitable. I felt it was now my fault he was going through more unnecessary pain.

I decided to pull the plug on life support. I sat overnight, talked with him, and said my goodbyes. My mother and aunt took my place so I could rest. I had only been gone a few hours, and he had passed.

I know this is not maybe what you signed up for when you purchased this book, but I think I needed to relay this information so you could understand what I went through next and why I felt what I felt. Remember I said I was also angry at myself when I was going through all that anger? I realized I was mad because some of me felt like I had killed my brother. It was my fault he was gone. I took him from his kids. I won't mention names, but someone had muttered this under their breath while passing me more than once, and I think those words set in. If someone close to me thinks it was my fault that my brother was dead, it was probably true. I believe this is where the guilt and remorse set in.

5

Remorse & The Sudden Attacks Of Grief

Guilt and remorse can make a combo attack on you so fast. Just knock you down from that power high you were feeling with all that anger. The guilt just started eating at me. I felt guilty for taking my brother off of life support. I felt that everyone was looking at me like I had murdered my brother. How could I do this? Didn't I love him? How could I do this to his kids? I am a horrible person. I don't deserve to be living my life. I would try to push those feelings away cause I knew my children still needed me.

I would get hit with another when I would get over one bout of guilt. I felt guilty for not being there for my brother more. I was guilty of trying to distance myself from him when he was sick. I knew his health was not doing good, but I felt like it was my fault. I could have taken care of him and forced him to be healthier. I could have found better doctors. The would have, could have, should have's were drowning me.

With the guilt and remorse came the Grief Attacks. These attacks would be uncontrollable crying, heart racing so fast I thought I was having a heart attack, the feeling like I couldn't catch my breath, and it would leave me feeling like I just ran a 5K. My mind would want to shut down, and I felt this heaviness with every movement I would make. I could be driving somewhere and get hit with a sudden grief attack. I would pull into a parking lot and let it all out. Sometimes they lasted a few minutes, and sometimes they lasted an hour. Anything could set them off. I was hearing our song playing on the radio, seeing someone that resembled him, hearing someone talking about their brother, or just receiving a call or a text from his children—watching my father grieve. He doesn't think he shows it, but it is there, and I can see it. Watching my mother lose her favorite child, the child she raised while she was still growing up herself. Watching her unravel was unbearable for me, and I could not go through it with her when I was already so shattered inside.

The guilt attacks and the depression that was winding its way through my head were starting to scare the shit out of me. I was afraid of what I might do to myself. I was scared of not being there for my children. I was worried I might have one of these attacks while driving with my kids and cause an accident. I knew I needed to do something, and I needed to start immediately.

II

Part Two

"Grief is not a disorder, a disease, or a sign of weakness. It is an emotional, physical, and spiritual necessity, the price you pay for love. The only cure for grief is to grieve."
Earl Grollman, as posted in **Living with Loss, Healing with Hope: A Jewish Perspective.**

6

FINDING YOUR WAY BACK

F inding my way back was not easy. I am optimistic it will be a unique journey for everyone. Finding your back is no easy task. It had to start with forgiving myself. I made it a habit to talk to myself every day. I promised not to speak negatively to myself anymore. I made it a chore to compliment myself every day when I woke up. Honestly, at first, I felt a bit stupid looking at myself in the mirror saying these things. I would even roll my eyes at myself at the start. After a bit of time, though, these little steps started to make a difference and gave me this glimmer of hope. These first steps allowed me to think positively about myself and start taking the steps I needed to forgive myself.

I was finally taking the time to acknowledge the pain, and with that came strength. I could openly start expressing my emotions and learn to work through them. I realized at this point that I had too much negativity in my life. I constantly had to deal with that on top of my grief. When I acknowledged pain and negativity in my life, this is when I started letting people go that were blocking me or getting in the way of reaching my peace. I am not saying start throwing everyone out of your life. I was just at a point in my life where it was either let people keep affecting my mental health and dragging me back to that breaking point or choose myself. I decided to love myself and put myself first; this was so hard because, to be honest, it was like I had lost someone else, but this was a choice I had to make. It was hard because it was not only affecting me but everyone else in my family.

Support was what I needed, and I found myself finally ready to ask for it. The time when saying I am fine, nothing is wrong with me is over. I reached out to my family (my sisters, husband, dad, and older sons.) I just needed that shoulder to cry on, someone to listen to how I felt. To vent and get it all out. Let them know when I needed the space to cry or lie down to think through my feelings. (Walking or hiking is suitable for this. I feel like that time to think things out while walking help, plus it releases the feel-good hormones.)

At this point, I started to see things around me differently. I still speak to my brother like he is still right next to me, and I don't think that will ever change. I believe that is one of the things that helped me get through the pain—feeling like he was right here with me. Whenever I see a hummingbird, I think, " Oh, here comes my brother to check on me. (Hummingbirds seem to be a thing that runs in my family) The day we were out looking at cemetery plots, a hummingbird kept following us from row to row. I see one from time to time in my backyard by my bedroom window. Then recently, when I went on vacation with my husband, I saw a hummingbird while we were sitting eating dinner at a restaurant on the patio. I looked over, smiled, and let out a little giggle. I thought, well, my brother decided to join me on my vacation. I have finally found peace and happiness. I have to work at keeping both still, and I still have myself a good cry from time to time. It just doesn't engulf me anymore. I cherish my memories of my brother and can now share them with him and my children. His memory will live on through me, and all that love him.

III

Part Three

"As long as I can, I will look at this world for both of us. As long as I can, I will laugh with the birds, I will sing with the flowers, I will pray to the stars for both of us."
Sascha, as posted in Chicken Soup for the Soul.

7

HONOR YOUR LOVED ONE

There are many ways to honor your loved one. I feel like when you find ways to celebrate your loved one; this helps give your life purpose again. I think when it is time for me to see my brother again. I need to have stories to tell him about the adventures I went on, how beautiful his children are, and to do this, I must live. I must live on, enjoy my life, and try new things even if they take me out of my comfort zone.

I have heard of many ways you can honor your loved one. I will share some of mine, no matter how silly you think they are. I watch Star Wars every year as that was something we had in common. I keep his computer chair even though it is a bit broken. It makes me feel like he is close to me. When I go to sleep, I say a little prayer hoping he hears me. (Prayer: Brother, if you can hear me, I love you and miss you. And I hope you know I did not steal your Ratt or Cinderella cassette tapes when we were kids. I did steal your Motley Crue tape, in my defense. I liked them more than you did. Good night brother.)

Here is a list of other ways I have heard of honoring a loved one:

- Making a quilt or pillow out of their clothing
- Donate to a charity in their name
- Start a scholarship in their name.
- Random acts of kindness on the anniversary of their passing or maybe on their birthday.
- Planting a tree or a flower garden as a memorial (Plant a garden &

the hummingbirds will come.)
- Start a tradition (I have a 4 ft Christmas tree that I put up that is solely dedicated to my brother, and I plan to add a new decoration to it every year. You better believe there are Star Wars ornaments on that tree.)
- Live your life fully. (I plan on doing this)

If these are not for you, there are many more online. Really so many, and maybe you will find something that fits you or just come up with something on your own.

8

TAKE YOU TIME: SELF-CARE

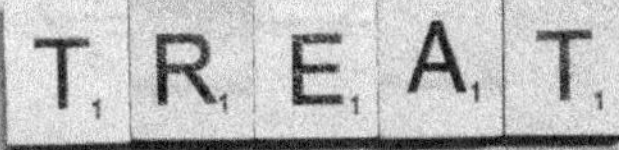
TREAT
YOURSELF
BETTER

I must stress that self-care is so important. Take time to yourself and adequately check in with yourself. When I say this, you ask yourself, how are you feeling? Do you need to pamper yourself a bit more? Do you need to take some quiet time? Do you need to get those feelings out on paper? Do you need to find someone you can talk with? These are valid questions; sometimes, you must stop or slow down. Life can get busy, and you start to place your focus on work or projects and forget to take care of yourself.

Here is a list of a few things I have found online or heard about through friends regarding self-care:

- Make sure to be kind to yourself. Love yourself
- Do something every day that brings you happiness (Pressing my Darth Vader bobblehead at work makes me smile while I am working, and when I am at home, my guilty pleasure is reading stories on Webtoons.)
- Express yourself: Journaling, meditation, music, art, or exercising. (As you may see, writing down my thoughts helps me express myself. It helps me work through whatever I am going through now.)
- Physical touch can help if you are distancing yourself from friends and family. Just the act of a hug or holding someone's hand can help calm or help release those overwhelming feelings you have been holding inside.
- Allow yourself to SLEEP. Sleep can be tricky, but you need this time to heal. Both your mind and body need the time to rest and recharge.
- Set a routine. Routine will bring structure back into your life and help keep you going when the grief is trying to pull you back in.
- Join a support group. A support system could make a massive difference in your life. I know not everyone has friends or family

they can rely on for support, so I suggest you search out a grief support group in your area.

- Finally, take care of your health. Shower, brush your teeth, eat healthier, and see your doctor. These are all very important to self-care.

I still struggle with self-care. I have always taken care of everyone else around me. I am a people pleaser. I usually put everyone else's needs first. So when days are hard, I still try to do the little things that make me happy. Remember to be kind to yourself, and the rest will follow.

9

Conclusion

Our journey through grief together has come to an end. I hope you have learned some things about grief and ways to start letting that peace and happiness back into your lives. This journey of writing out my struggles and reliving the suffering has been cathartic for me. I hope you realize you are not alone. I thank you for coming along with me. I wish you all the luck on your journey.

If you made it to the end of my story and found this book helpful, I would be grateful if you left a positive review for the book on AMAZON!

10

Resources

elinda Smith, M.A., Lawrence Robinson, And Jeanne Segal, Ph.D. (2021, October 1). *Coping with Grief and Loss.* HelpGuide.Org. Retrieved August 6, 2022, from https://www.helpguide.org/articles/grief/coping-with-grief-and-loss.htm

IRVING, W. (2021, January 1). [QUOTE]. Https://Www.Mygriefassist.Com.Au/Inspiration-Resources/Quotes/. https://www.mygriefassist.com.au/inspiration-resources/quotes/

Grollman, E. A. (2001). *Living with Loss, Healing with Hope: A Jewish Perspective.* Beacon Press.

Newmark, A., & Geiger, A. T. (2014). *Chicken Soup for the Soul: Living with Alzheimerâs & Other Dementias.* Chicken Soup for the Soul.

Empathy's Grief Specialists. (2020b). *Feeling Numb After Someone You Love Dies.* Www.Empathy.Com. Retrieved August 6, 2022, from https://www.empathy.com/grief/feeling-numb-after-a-loss

Kenneth J. Doka, Ph.D., MDiv, Hospice Foundation of America. (2012). *Anger and Grief*. Www.HospiceFoundation.Org. Retrieved August 6, 2022, from https://hospicefoundation.org/End-of-Life-Support-and-Resources/Grief-Support/Journeys-with-Grief-Articles/Anger-and-G rief

Betcher, B. (2018, March 2). *9 Ways To Honor A Loved One That Has Passed*. CaringBridge.Org. Retrieved August 7, 2022, from https://ww w.caringbridge.org/resources/9-ways-remember-loved-one-passed/

Altru.org. (2019, August 2). *20 Ways To Take Care Of Yourself While Grieving*. Retrieved August 7, 2022, from https://www.altru.org/blog/ 2019/august/20-ways-to-take-care-of-yourself-while-grieving/